Ripley's Believe It or Not!

Developed and produced by Ripley Publishing Ltd

This edition published and distributed by:
Mason Crest Publishers Inc.
370 Reed Road, Broomall, Pennsylvania 19008
(866) MCP-BOOK (toll free)
www.masoncrest.com

Ripley's Believe it or Not!
The Final Reckoning
ISBN 978-1-4222-2020-7 (hardcover)
ISBN 978-1-4222-2054-2 (paperback)

Library of Congress Cataloging-in-Publication data is available

Ripley's Believe it or Not!—Complete 16 Title Series
ISBN 978-1-4222-2014-6

1st printing
10 9 8 7 6 5 4 3 2 1

Library of Congress Cataloging-in-Publication Data is available.
Printed in USA

PUBLISHER'S NOTE
While every effort has been made to verify the accuracy of the entries in this book, the Publisher's cannot be held responsible for any errors contained in the work. They would be glad to receive any information from readers.

WARNING
Some of the stunts and activities in this book are undertaken by experts and should not be attempted by anyone without adequate training and supervision.

Expect... The Unexpected

Mason Crest Publishers

THE FINAL RECKONING

Just when you thought you couldn't take any

more, this off-the-wall book gives you another

helping. Get to know the two-year-old pet lion,

the villagers who dress as heads on plates for their

annual carnival, and the floating wooden Ferrari

that drives around Venice.

This soft, leather flying jacket may look
authentic but it is actually made from wood...

Full of ENteRprise

TONY ALLEYNE has boldly gone where no interior designer has gone before by converting his apartment into a replica of the starship *Enterprise*.

Star Trek fan Tony, from Hinckley, England, watched hours of *Star Trek* videos to help him recreate the transporter console from the *Enterprise.* When he was unable to find a home for it, he redesigned his apartment to accommodate it.

Between 1999 and 2004, he worked to give the small apartment a futuristic feel, complete with voice-activated lighting, realistic console panels, and an infinity mirror above the toilet. Where most people have a bedroom, Tony has a replica of the transporter unit that beams crew members to far-flung locations. Speakers in the rooms replay sound effects from *Star Trek*, and there is a cardboard cutout of Patrick Stewart as Capt. Jean-Luc Picard, the commander from *Star Trek: The Next Generation.* "If you're going to do something, you have to go all the way," says Tony.

Tony and the cardboard cutout of Capt. Jean-Luc Picard in his main living room space, which also houses his transporter console.

Every detail, from this screen, which faces into the kitchen, to the windows of the apartment, follows the Star Trek theme.

Tony in his converted kitchen, complete with futuristic white units and specialist lighting underneath the cupboards.

These panels show Alleyne's amazing craftsmanship, as well as his fidelity to the Star Trek original.

◀ **Pencil Passion**
Emanuel Petran from the Czech Republic has collected an amazing 3,333 pencils over a period of almost 30 years. He plans to combine his collection with another to form a museum dedicated to the graphite wooden pencil.

Horn Haul

A Chinese pensioner can lift up to 14 bricks with a "horn" that has grown on his forehead. When doctors told him that they couldn't operate on the tumor—which is 2 in (5 cm) long—because of its location, 74-year-old Wang Ying decided to incorporate it into the strong-man act he had been performing since the age of eight. He lifts the bricks by means of a length of rope looped around the protruding facial growth.

Escape Relay

In October 2005, more than 50 escapologists in different venues, from Australia to California, took part in the Worldwide Escape Artist Relay—the largest ever coordinated performance by escape artists. One of the most daring feats was that of Paul Sautzer (a.k.a. Dr. Wilson) who, in Mount Desert Island, Maine, escaped from a combination of padlocks, manacles, and chains, and an iron collar called the Chrysalis.

Sketch Wizard

George Vlosich III, of Lakewood, Ohio, produces detailed portraits of famous people—from The Beatles to baseball star Mickey Mantle—all on an Etch-a-Sketch®. He spends up to 100 hours on each picture and sells the best as unique works of art. He has even had an Etch-a-Sketch® signed by President Clinton.

Human Robot

A Japanese company has enabled human movement to be operated by remote control. A headset sends a low-voltage current through the wearer's head, affecting the nerves that help maintain balance.

Full Facial

Three teams of scientists, from the U.S.A., France, and Egypt, have created incredibly detailed facial reconstructions of the ancient Egyptian king, Tutankhamun. The teams each built a model of the young Pharaoh's face, based on approximately 1,700 high-resolution images taken from CT scans of his mummy. They reveal what King Tut looked like on the day he died, nearly 3,300 years ago. The scans, which are the first ever of an Egyptian mummy, suggest that he was a healthy, yet slightly built 19-year-old, standing 5 ft 6 in (1.67 m) tall.

Boy Racer

While his father was in a store buying a chocolate bar, three-year-old Oliver Willment-Coster, of Bournemouth, England, managed to release the handbrake of the family car, take the car out of neutral, and steer it one-handed down the street, until he smashed into a parked police van.

Oliver had been strapped into the passenger seat of his father's car when he managed to drive off.

Field Trials

Nova Scotia farmer Andrew Rand proposed to his girlfriend by hopping onto a tractor and using a plow to carve the words "LISE MARRY ME" in huge letters in a rye field. His efforts probably inspired Chris Mueller from North Dakota to use a plow to pop the question to Katie Goltz in a soybean field. He had almost finished his message when he realized there wasn't enough room for all the letters. Fortunately, "Katie will you M-A-R-Y me?" still won her heart when she viewed it from the air.

Married 162 Times

Believe it or not, a 75-year-old Bosnian man claimed to have married 162 times! Nedeljko Ilincic said he first got married when he was 15 and since then it has been "just one wife after another."

Lawful Wedded Dolphin

In 2005, Sharon Tendler married Cindy the dolphin at a special ceremony in Eilat, Israel. She got down on one knee and gave Cindy a kiss and a piece of herring. Sharon met Cindy 15 years ago and has since visited the dolphin two or three times a year.

Hanging Around

Scottish artist David Mach has definitely got the hang of sculpture—he makes lifelike models out of wire coat hangers! First he makes a plastic mold of the model shape, around which he shapes the coat hangers. Each coat hanger is individually formed and bent, then welded several times to its neighbor. He leaves the hooks protruding out to create a ghostly fuzz around the object, which he says gives the final sculpture a kind of aura and makes it more enticing to look at.

Depressing Date

Psychological researchers in the U.K. claim that January 24 is the most depressing day of the year.

A TOKYO department store has a pair of slippers inspired by the **Wizard of Oz**. They glisten with **690 rubies** and are worth **$2 million!**

Odd Love

When political activist Regina Kaiser was arrested at her Berlin apartment in 1981 and taken to the Communist Stasi security police headquarters for questioning, she feared the worst. However, to her surprise, she fell in love with her interrogator, Uwe Karlstedt, and the couple are still together 25 years later.

▶ A Lot of Hot Air

Hot-air balloons prepare to take off (left) at an air base in Chambley, northern France, on July 23, 2005. The 261 balloons lined both sides of the road as they aimed to float into the air at the same time—and in a line.

Tenpin Pong

For the bowler who can sniff victory, Storm Products, based in Brigham City, Utah, manufactures a range of scented bowling balls, including cinnamon, orange, amaretto, and cherry. They cost between $150 and $250.

Ice-cream salesman **Derek Greenwood,** of ROCHDALE, ENGLAND, had a *funeral procession* that consisted of **12 ice-cream vans** all playing jingles on their way to the cemetery!

Surprised Patriarch

Mick Henry of Yorkshire, England, discovered at the age of 59 that he is a tribal chief of the Ojibway Tribe of Manitoba, Canada.

Big Order

After Gita, a 47-year-old Asian elephant, resident at Los Angeles Zoo, California, had infected portions of a toe removed from her left front foot in September 2005, orthopedic shoemaker Cesar Lua was asked to create a boot to keep the wound clean while it healed. Working from photographs and measurements supplied by the zoo, Lua took a full 12 hours to craft the $450 circular shoe. Made mostly of brown leather, ½ in (1 cm) thick, the finished shoe measured 53 in (135 cm) in circumference and 19 in (48 cm) in diameter. It was held to the elephant's ankle by means of a strap.

Alcatraz Swim

A nine-year-old boy succeeded in 2005 where many before had failed—by escaping from Alcatraz. In October 2005, Johnny Wilson, from Hillsborough, California, swam 1.4 mi (2.2 km) from the island to San Francisco in less than two hours to raise money for the victims of Hurricane Katrina.

Hippo Sweat

In 2005, Professor Christopher Viney, of the University of California, collected and studied hippopotamus sweat, hoping that the ingredients would help develop new human sunscreens!

WOLF BOYS

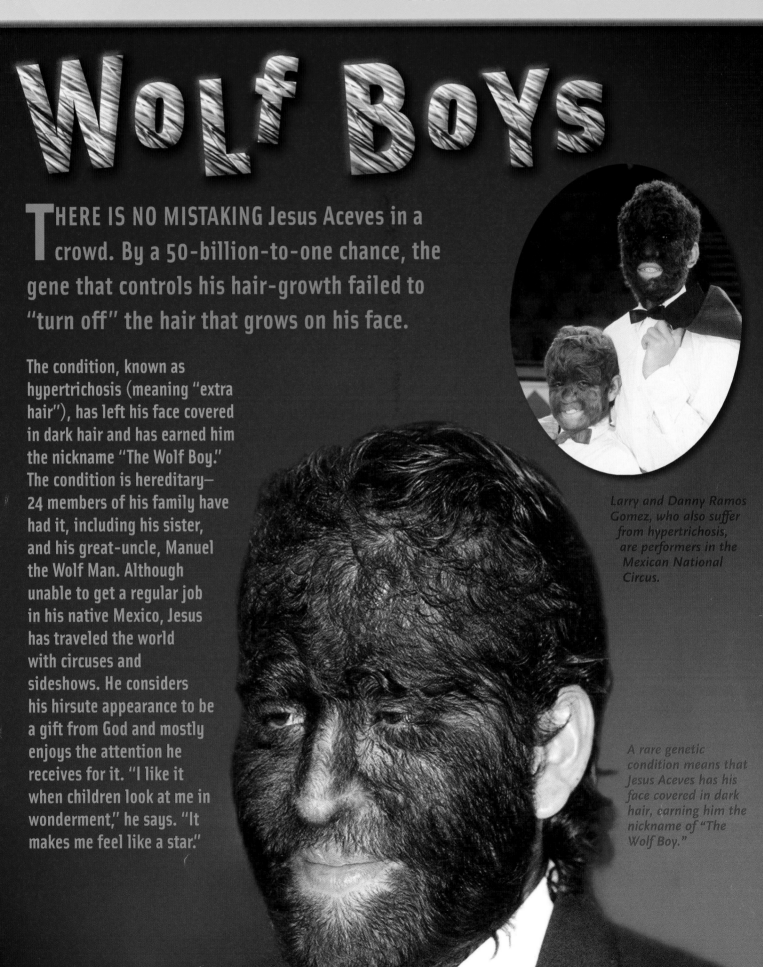

THERE IS NO MISTAKING Jesus Aceves in a crowd. By a 50-billion-to-one chance, the gene that controls his hair-growth failed to "turn off" the hair that grows on his face.

The condition, known as hypertrichosis (meaning "extra hair"), has left his face covered in dark hair and has earned him the nickname "The Wolf Boy." The condition is hereditary— 24 members of his family have had it, including his sister, and his great-uncle, Manuel the Wolf Man. Although unable to get a regular job in his native Mexico, Jesus has traveled the world with circuses and sideshows. He considers his hirsute appearance to be a gift from God and mostly enjoys the attention he receives for it. "I like it when children look at me in wonderment," he says. "It makes me feel like a star."

Larry and Danny Ramos Gomez, who also suffer from hypertrichosis, are performers in the Mexican National Circus.

A rare genetic condition means that Jesus Aceves has his face covered in dark hair, earning him the nickname of "The Wolf Boy."

Ear Hole
Venezuelan tattoo-artist Constantino has stretched his earlobe so much that he can place a shot glass in it.

Screw Loose
When Etienne Verhees, from Antwerp, Belgium, started coughing in October 2005, he coughed up a metal screw! It was one of four screws that had been used to hold a metal plate in place in his neck after he had broken two vertebrae falling from a ladder in 2001. Doctors said that the screw must have moved following an infection.

Linda Dagless and **Brad Wheeler,** of NORWICH, ENGLAND, named their baby daughter "**Ikea**" after the Swedish furniture company!

Potter Potty
Fifteen-year-old Harry Potter fan Sandra Luchian, from Moldova, spent over a month of her 2005 summer vacation writing out the latest book, because she couldn't afford to buy it. She borrowed a copy of *Harry Potter and the Half-Blood Prince* from a friend and wrote down the 607-page story word for word in five notebooks.

Giant Bunny
Visitors to a northern Italian mountain could be forgiven for thinking they were seeing things. In 2005, a huge pink rabbit was erected on the side of the 5,000-ft (1,524-m) high Colletto Fava mountain. The soft toy, which is 200 ft (61 m) long, is expected to stay in place until 2025, and was designed by Austrian artists.

Dead Chrysler
Angry because his car wouldn't start, a Florida man pulled out a gun and shot it! John McGivney fired five rounds into the hood of his Chrysler outside his home in Fort Lauderdale. When startled neighbors asked him what he was doing, he calmly replied: "I'm putting my car out of its misery."

Touch Test
A blind German woman can distinguish between colors simply by touch. Gabriele Simon, from Wallenhorst, uses her fingertips to recognize the different colors of various items of clothing. She says it has taken her 20 years to master the skill, which gives her greater independence, as she no longer has to ask her mother what to wear.

Free-falling
"Jump for the Cause," a nonprofit organization that specializes in skydiving fund-raisers, succeeded in performing an amazing 151-person formation skydive. The skydivers were made up of women from 24 different U.S. states, 15 different countries, and varied occupations.

Greedy Thief
A 308-lb (140-kg) thief, who ransacked a pie store near Fagaras, Romania, was caught after getting stuck on his way out. When the owner arrived to open the store the following morning, he found a pair of legs hanging out of the window!

Fake Cow Stolen

Believe it or not, a full-size, fiberglass cow was stolen from a roadside billboard in eastern Virginia, in October 2005. One of a pair valued at $3,200, the 500-lb (227-kg) black-and-white cow was removed from the billboard along Interstate 464 in Chesapeake.

Love Letters

Every year, in the build-up to February 14, the tiny post office in the small Texas town of Valentine becomes one of the busiest in the world. Postmaster Maria Elena Carrasco and her lone part-time assistant suddenly have to deal with a flood of mail as more than 7,000 romantics, from all corners of the globe, dispatch cards to be stamped with the postmark of Valentine.

Queasy Rider

Millard Dwyer from Pulaski County, Kentucky, was fined $225 in 2005 for "driving" a horse under the influence of alcohol. Dwyer, who was stopped by police as he tried to steer his horse Prince around a street corner, was three times over the legal limit after downing a 12-pack of beer. Kentucky state law classes a horse as a vehicle.

Foxy Thief

After frolicking in the waves in the summer of 2005, beachgoers on Prince Edward Island, Canada, returned to the shore only to find that their sandals had been stolen—by a marauding family of foxes.

Unplanned Landing

On a forced landing, Mark and Mercedes Davies landed their single-engine plane atop a moving semi-truck before crashing onto the highway. Incredibly, both of them emerged unharmed!

Roses are Red

★ For Valentine's Day 2005, Brazilian teenager Frederico Skwara bought girlfriend Juliana Magalhaes a pregnant sheep called Waffle.

★ Special "flirt" carriages were created on the subway in Vienna, Austria, for Valentine's Day 2003, to encourage all single passengers to find love.

★ The most popular Valentine's gifts in China are not chocolates or flowers, but tropical fish!

Testing Times

Seo Sang-moon finally passed the academic part of his driver's licence examination in South Korea in 2005—on the 272nd attempt.

Walking Underwater

Lloyd Scott, from Rainham, England, completed a marathon underwater (26.2 mi/42.2 km) starting in Lochend, Scotland, in October 2003, while wearing a lead-booted early diving suit weighing 120 lb (54 kg). It took him 12 days to finish the walk, emerging at Loch Ness.

Served-up Heads!
Villagers dressed as heads on plates during the New Year's Carnival in the village of Vevcani, Macedonia, in 2006. The 1,300-year-old carnival features the villagers performing in a variety of events.

Whopper Chopper
Mark Henry is altogether a little young to be long in the tooth. But the nine-year-old Canadian stunned dentists with a top right front tooth that measured nearly 1 in (2.5 cm) long. Dr. Gabriela Gandila of Owen Sound, Ontario, who had to pull out the tooth, said it was like a horse's.

The Quicker Flicker
In August 2005, Sheeshpal Agarwal was officially declared the fastest dentures remover in India. The 51-year-old can remove and reinsert his teeth with a single flick of his tongue 176 times in 5 minutes.

Wide Awake
Silvio Jarquin Rostran and Janeth Margarita Cerrato from Nicaragua won a no-sleep marathon in 2005 by staying awake for 51 hours.

Believe it or not, a **100-year-old** Belgian motorist, **Cyriel Delacauw**, was given an **insurance discount** in 2005 because he **hadn't** had an **accident** in more than **80 years** of driving!

Lying Low
A 6-ft (1.8-m) tall man on the run from police was found four months later in a bizarre hideout—curled up inside a TV set in a mobile home near Bainbridge, Georgia. The fugitive had escaped from Florida police in September 2004.

Cheerers' Chant
A man who left the scene of a road accident in Ann Arbor, Michigan, in August 2005, was tracked down, not by police but by local cheerleaders. Members of the Lincoln High School varsity cheerleading squad witnessed the crash and turned the man's licence plate number into a cheer so that they would be able to remember it.

Car Possessed
We've all heard of cars being repossessed, but Christine Djordjevic is convinced that her car is possessed. In March 2005, the driverless vehicle started itself and reversed into a neighbor's home, at South Haven, Indiana, causing damage worth several thousand dollars. Police officers were sceptical of the story until they saw the 1995 Mercury Tracer Trio start itself again and head down the road. They stopped it before it hit anything.

GLoWiNG PiGs

WHAT'S GREEN, grunts and glows in the dark? A Taiwanese pig, of course!

Scientists in Taiwan have bred three fluorescent green pigs by adding genetic material from jellyfish into normal pig embryos. Although other countries have created partially fluorescent pigs, these are the first to be green from the inside out. Even each pig's heart and internal organs are green.

DNA from jellyfish was added to around 265 pig embryos, which were implanted in eight different sows. Four of the female pigs became pregnant and gave birth to three green male piglets in 2005.

Two years earlier, Taiwanese scientists had created the world's first glowing green fish. Now researchers hope that the pigs will be able to help in the study of stem cell research to combat human diseases.

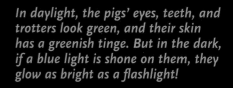

In daylight, the pigs' eyes, teeth, and trotters look green, and their skin has a greenish tinge. But in the dark, if a blue light is shone on them, they glow as bright as a flashlight!

Making a Splash

Underwater hockey was invented in 1954 by field hockey players looking for a way to keep fit during winter. Here, a team from Roger Bacon High School in Cincinnati, Ohio, take on Michigan State University in a nationals match.

Isak and the Beanstalk

When nine-year-old Isak Spanjol planted a squash seed in the family yard in Brooklyn, New York, in 2004, he had no idea that it would grow into a monster plant. The rare species of gourd coiled around cable lines and stretched over fences into neighboring yards. Some of the vegetables hanging from it were 6½ ft (2 m) long, nearly 2 ft (0.6 m) bigger than the botanist himself!

Driving Green

Mali Blotta and David Modersbach drove 11,000 mi (17,700 km) from California to Argentina in 2004, in a station wagon that ran on recycled vegetable oil instead of gas!

Prize Pumpkin

When Ron and Sue Boor paraded their prize pumpkin at the 2005 West Virginia Pumpkin Festival, it took five men and a forklift to get it onto the scales! The Boors, who have been raising large pumpkins since 1990, had produced a 1,082-lb (492-kg) monster. At its peak, the pumpkin grew 35 lb (16 kg) a night and "drank" 198 gal (750 l) of water a day.

Self-healing

Pedro Lopez, a 39-year-old Mexican, amazed physicians by successfully performing complex surgery on himself. By inserting a needle through his navel, he drained fluid from his lungs that was hampering his breathing. Specialists described it as a miracle. "We do this kind of surgery draining liquid in small quantities," said one, "but this man drained three liters of liquid—and without anesthesia!"

Young Juror

Nathaniel Skiles, of Kirkland, Washington, has been summoned for jury duty three times in two years—and he's only six years old! The blunder occurred after his birthdate was listed incorrectly on a state identification card.

Jumbo Treadmill

Finding that Maggie, an African elephant, was 1,000 lb (454 kg) overweight, officials at the Alaska Zoo introduced a specially made treadmill to help her exercise off the excess pounds. The treadmill is 20 ft (6 m) long, 8 ft (2.4 m) wide, and weighs 15,972 lb (7,244 kg). It is believed to be the first treadmill in the world built specifically for an elephant.

Late Mail

Evelyn Greenawald, of Anamosa, Iowa, received a postcard from her daughter Sheri in Germany in October 2005—27 years after it had been mailed. At the time of writing the postcard, Sheri was beginning her opera career in Europe. She now lives in San Francisco, California.

Cookie Lady

Merry Debbrecht, of Rose Hill, Kansas, has been baking up to 480 cookies a day and sending them to U.S. soldiers who are stationed in Iraq. By the summer of 2005, she had sent more than 30,000 cookies and said that she wouldn't stop until the war was over.

Seal of Disapproval

A man from Colorado was arrested in 2004 when he tried to board a plane at Logan Airport, Boston, Massachusetts, carrying the severed head of a seal. Security staff discovered the head in a small canvas cooler.

Bike Tree

Most people keep their Harley motorcycle on the driveway or in the garage. But Richard Woodworth keeps his in a tree outside his home in Raleigh, North Carolina. He insists that hanging the bike from the branches is art.

After a **television** belonging to **Chris van Rossman,** of CORVALLIS, Oregon, began emitting an international satellite **distress signal**, police and military **rescue units** showed up to save it!

Name Game

A man called Pete set up a website in 2005 with the aim of getting another 1,999 Petes to attend a gathering in London, England! Pete Trainor started his quest as a bet.

Ghost Guard

Dave Davison has one of America's most unusual jobs—he guards a bonafide ghost town. Built during the late-19th century by prospectors looking for silver and gold, Silver City, Idaho, is a ghost town in the winter. Its 40 homes (which are owned by summer vacationers) become deserted and the town is usually cut off by road from the outside world because of snow. As watchman, Davison thwarts thieves on snowmobiles to ensure that Silver City doesn't disappear from the map altogether.

Pretty in Pink

When 700 prisoners had to walk 2 mi (3.2 km) to be transferred from their old overcrowded jail to a brand new, bigger facility in Phoenix, Arizona, in 2005, Sheriff Joe Arpaio came up with a surefire way to prevent the convicts from escaping—he dressed them in fluffy pink underwear and flip-flops! He reckoned that the hardened criminals would simply be too embarrassed to run.

◄ *Flip-Flop Sculpture*
Australian John Dahlsen puts the finishing touch to his sculpture made from hundreds of flip-flops on Sydney's Bondi Beach in 2004 as part of the "Sculptures by the Sea" exhibition. Dahlsen scours Australian beaches for plastic objects washed up by the ocean to make into artworks.

WRITTEN IN SKIN
Rosa Barthelme of Kansas picked up the name "The Human Slate" because messages written lightly on her skin stood out and remained for about 30 minutes.

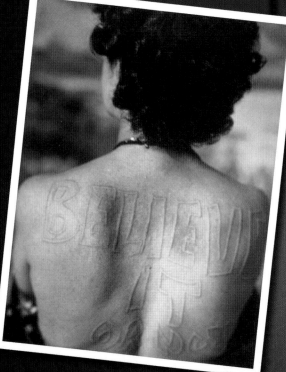

WHAT A HANDFUL!
Julius B. Shuster, of Pennsylvania, perfected the art of holding 20 baseballs in one hand!

OPEN PRISON
People of the city of Anna Maria, Florida, were so proud of their lack of crime that they bragged their jail had no bars, roof, doors, or windows.

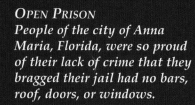

LARGE LUMP
This 6,725-lb (3,050-kg) piece of solid coal from Dawson, New Mexico, was paraded proudly at a Cowboys Reunion on July 4, 1930.

CROSS-LOG SKIING
The log-packed Androscoggin River was crossed in 1955 by Kenneth Lambert on a pair of snow skis.

FAMILY TRANSPORT
In 1938, the Harriman family rode from Portland, Oregon, to Toledo, Ohio, on a motorcycle. The total weight of the four people and their dog was 590 lb (268 kg).

WELL RISEN
In Ravenna, Kentucky, a well that had previously been sunk into the ground gradually rose out of it. By 1932, it had risen 8 ft (2.4 m) above the earth.

OFFICE PET
Mrs. Brodie's boss, although a car dealer by day, was also a game hunter. Mrs. Brodie is pictured here in 1941 with a tame lion that her boss captured as a cub, and whom she raised in her office.

Looking Back

April 29, 1927 **Bobby Leach**, who survived going over Niagara Falls in a barrel in 1911, died from injuries received when he slipped on a banana skin while walking along the street.

December 2, 1927 Little **Marie Finster** jumped from the roof of a building and was saved miraculously by falling into her mother's arms, who happened to be passing at that very minute.

Toilet Snake

Going to the bathroom will never be the same for Alicia Bailey of Jacksonville, Florida—not since she was bitten by a venomous snake hiding in her toilet bowl. As she lifted the toilet lid, a water moccasin bit her on the leg. She survived the ordeal, but admitted that she had become "toilet shy."

Hopelessly Lost

In 2005, three elderly U.S. ladies took 24 hours to get home after becoming lost on their 20-mi (32-km) journey home from church. What should have been a short drive to Upson County, Florida, turned into an A.P.B. from worried relatives, as 72-year-old Alice Atwater took Florence King and Ruthelle Outler on an unintentional detour through Birmingham, Alabama, and the Georgia cities of Atlanta and Macon.

Mature Mother

Adriana Iliescu, aged 67, claimed to be the oldest recorded woman to give birth. A university professor and children's author from Bucharest, Romania, Adriana gave birth to a daughter after doctors reversed the effects of menopause. They then used in-vitro fertilization and the sperm and eggs from younger people to impregnate her.

Adriana Iliescu with her one-year-old daughter Eliza Maria, on January 16, 2006.

Stop Thief!

Having cut through a security fence at a shop in Durham, North Carolina, in 2005, a thief stole 50 red, octagonal stop signs valued at $1,250. He was arrested after being spotted pushing a shopping cart filled with signs and trying to sell 16 of them for $28.

Blooming Great!

In Vienna, West Virginia, Brenda Wilson lovingly tends a rosebush that just won't stop growing. The bush was planted in 1966 and stands more than 16 ft (4.9 m) tall—over four times the usual height for a rose bush.

◀ Extra Tongue

Delores Whittington's cat is truly unique in the feline world. Not only was she born with five toes on each paw (hence her name Five Toes), but the black Burmese mix also has two tongues! Delores, from Dobson, North Carolina, noticed the twin tongues for the first time back in December 2004.

Hiss-terical

A woman was attacked by a 4-ft (1.2-m) long python while watching a movie at a cinema in the United Arab Emirates, in June 2005. A friend uncoiled the snake from the hysterical woman's leg and removed the serpent from the cinema. Both women continued watching the film.

Believe it or not, **Stormy**, a *groundhog* at CHICAGO'S BROOKFIELD ZOO, had braces fitted to his **lower teeth** in 2005 to enable them to **grow straight** and help him eat!

Odd One Out

Debby Cantlon, from Seattle, Washington, couldn't help noticing that there was something unusual about one of the pups being fed by Mademoiselle Giselle, her Papillon dog. The strange "pup" was actually an orphaned newborn squirrel, who was happily being allowed to feed from the dog right alongside its canine "brothers and sisters."

Big Knit

By the spring of 2007, Darlene Rouse hopes to have knitted a scarf that is a mile long! With help from a close-knit group of friends and family in Opelika, Alabama, she has been working on the inspirational Hope Scarf, a garment that will carry each knitter's name, along with a short, life-affirming message.

Mother Love

Reggie the hamadryas baboon was the star attraction at England's Paignton Zoo in 2005—but for all the wrong reasons. After being born with a normal covering of hair on his head, Reggie had it all licked off by his overly attentive mother, leaving one bald baby baboon!

Smoking Chimp

A chimpanzee at a zoo in China has finally managed to quit smoking—after 16 years of nicotine addiction. Ai Ai, a 27-year-old chimp at Qinling Safari Park, started smoking cigarettes given to her by visitors after her mate died in 1989. When a second mate died and her daughter was moved to another zoo in 1997, the lonely Ai Ai began chain-smoking. Worried about her deteriorating health, keepers tried to get her to kick the habit by giving her earphones and allowing her to listen to music on a Sony Walkman. At first Ai Ai still squealed for cigarettes but, ultimately captivated by her new interest, she soon forgot about her smoking habit altogether.

A Bit Cheesy!

Room 114 at the Washington Jefferson Hotel in New York City was redecorated by the artist Cosimo Cavallaro, in May 1999, using 1,000 lb (454 kg) of melted cheese! Cavallaro explained that he did it to show his joy for life. The installation of "cheese art" remained on display for a month.

Rock Champions

One of Canada's more unusual sporting events is the Rock Paper Scissors World Championships, held in Toronto. Although originally a children's game, there are now more than 2,200 members of the World Rock Paper Scissors Society, and players travel to Toronto from Oslo, Prague, Sydney, London, and all over the U.S.A. The victor collects $7,000 in prize money.

Hamster Power

A 16-year-old boy from Somerset, England, invented a hamster-powered cellular phone! Peter Ash attached a generator to the exercise wheel of Elvis the hamster and connected it to his phone charger. He said: "Every two minutes Elvis spends on his wheel gives me around 30 minutes of talk time on my phone."

Lucky Jim

Jim McClatchey died 100 times on November 20, 2004, but still came back to life! Doctors at the Piedmont Hospital, Atlanta, Georgia, were stunned as McClatchey suffered repeated cardiac arrests needing immediate shock treatment. In the first hour alone, his heart stopped 50 times. He had to be shocked so frequently that he sustained second-degree burns to his chest.

Hard Cheese

A year after intentionally sinking 1,760 lb (800 kg) of cheese into the water off the Saguenay fjord, north of Quebec City, Canada, a cheese company finally gave up hope of its recovery when divers and high-tech tracking equipment failed to locate it to bring it back to the surface. Leaving the $50,000 cheese in 160 ft (50 m) of water for months was supposed to produce a unique flavor.

Jackpot!

Once jailed for lottery fraud, when freed, Romanian Stancu Ogica won $33,000 playing the lottery!

Christmas Bonus

In December 2004, Richard and Donna Hamann paid that month's electric bill for all of Anthon, Iowa!

Heart Beats

★ A human heart beats 100,000 times a day, and during an average lifetime it will beat more than 2.5 billion times.

★ Blood pumped out from your heart travels 60,000 mi (96,560 km) around your body each day—that's 20 times the distance across the U.S.A. from coast to coast.

★ The human heart pumps about one million barrels of blood during an average lifetime—enough to fill more than three super-tankers.

⊙ Metal Skyline

Chinese artist Zhan Wang chose kitchen utensils as his medium to recreate London's urban landscape. He even included a dry ice machine to give the work an atmospheric London fog.

Junior Filmmaker

Nine-year-old Kishen from Bangalore, India, made history in 2005 by directing a full-length feature film. The movie is called *Care of Footpath* and is about slum children. Kishen has been acting since the age of four and has appeared in 24 movies and more than 1,000 TV shows.

Chat Tomb

Driven by a desire to speak to his late mother, Juergen Broether from Germany has devised a $1,940 mobile phone and loudspeaker device that can be buried next to a coffin. The device enables people to talk to the dead for up to a year.

Home Is Where Your Car Is

After being evicted from her London, England, home, Ann Naysmith lived in her car for 26 years. When health inspectors confiscated her old Ford, community members bought her a Mercedes!

IN DEPTH
Cannon Fodder

Missouri daredevil David "The Bullet" Smith calls himself a "human cannonball" and is blasted from his cannon 500 times a year worldwide.

How did you become a human cannonball?

" My parents were circus performers and my father David Smith Sr. became a human cannonball himself more than 30 years ago. All of my nine siblings have done it, and when I was 17 my father said I was ready. A year or so later he hurt his back and asked me to stand in for him, and that was that. "

What happens when you are "fired?"

" I can't tell you how the cannon is ignited—it's a family secret. But there is a tremendous force on my body—10 Gs, which is ten times my bodyweight. I start off at the bottom of the 34-ft-long barrel—before I get to the end I've already traveled 30 ft. I then go from 0 to 50 mph in a fifth of a second. The whole flight of about 150 ft takes under 4 seconds. "

How do you land?

" I fly about 80 ft up in the air, somersault, and land on my back in a net which is usually about 20 x 50 ft big. "

What do you feel when you are in the air?

" I'm very aware—it's like slow motion. I think about what direction the wind is hitting me from, where my netting is, whether I need to correct my flight path, if I have clearance of obstacles above, and below me. I even occasionally wonder what we're having for dinner! It all happens so fast, my mind's just along for the ride. "

What unusual places have you been fired over?

" I was shot over part of the Grand Canyon. I also shoot over Ferris wheels, and was once shot into slime for a world record. I stood in for Ewan McGregor in Tim Burton's movie Big Fish. "

Who makes your cannons?

" My father has built seven cannons himself. I'm just putting the wheels on my first. We've got cannons ranging from 18 ft long to 36 ft. "

Does your father still perform?

" Yes, he's 63. He was recently shot from Tijuana, Mexico, into the U.S.A.—the first person to be shot over an international border. He held his passport in his hands as he went. We also once performed in cannons side by side—I broke my father's previous distance record as I came out, and he landed one second later and broke mine. He holds the current record of 201 ft 4 in. "

Does it hurt—and have you had any injuries?

" It hurts your whole body. I've never missed the net—I wouldn't expect to live through that. I did blast a hole in the net once—I woke up eight minutes later surrounded by paramedics, but miraculously I wasn't badly injured. "

Will your own young daughters follow you into the act?

" My six-year-old isn't interested, but my youngest is nearly two and is a daredevil, so she might. Her mother would shoot me—but then she shoots me anyway: she pulls the trigger on the cannon! "

www.humancannonball.us

The Bullet

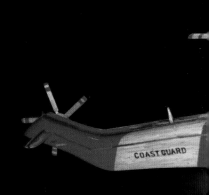

ONE OF RIPLEY'S latest museums, Key West, opened in 2003. Among its varied unbelievable exhibits are a Jivaro Indian shrunken torso, once owned by Ernest Hemingway, and a portrait of Vincent van Gogh made from butterfly wings.

PHURBU DAGGER
Tibetan monks use these daggers to exorcise evil spirits.

RAMA STATUE
This Thai statue of Rama, a Hindu god, was set in rice fields to assure a good harvest.

DON'T MISS!

▶ Collection of multi-leaf clovers

▶ Giant tree-climbing coconut crab

▶ Spiked torture chair

▶ Human bone rosary

▶ Toast art: "Adam" (from Michelangelo's Creation)

▶ Woman's bolero cape made from human hair

▶ A pair of gold lamé panties autographed by Madonna

▶ Three-legged chicken

MASTODON SKULL
The Mastodon is a prehistoric relative of the elephant—its tusks were up to 10 ft (3 m) long.

MATCHSTICK MODEL
Made by a prisoner serving a life sentence since 1979 in England.

FANTASY COFFIN
In Ghana, coffins reflect the status of the deceased. Paa Joe carved this lobster coffin.

GUMBALL PORTRAIT
Chewing one gumball a day, it would take you 27 years to chew the 10,000 gumballs used to make this portrait of Robert Ripley.

EXECUTIONER'S SWORD
Ripley brought this weapon from China where it was used to behead criminals.

CANNIBAL SKULL
Now extremely rare, cannibal trophy skulls used to be worn as amulets by warriors in New Guinea.

Wood You Believe It!

THE RESIDENTS OF VENICE are used to watching gondolas navigating the city's famous network of canals, but to see a Ferrari floating along the waterways is a different matter altogether.

But this is no ordinary car—it is made entirely from wood, right down to the steering wheel, upholstery, and mirrors. The Ferrari F50 is one of several full-size wooden cars created by Italian artist Livio De Marchi, a man who combines skill, wit, and panache to design lifelike sculptures from wood.

This soft, leather flying jacket may look authentic, but it's actually made from the same material as the hanger—wood.

In De Marchi's bathroom is a wooden dress that has been "washed and hung up to dry."

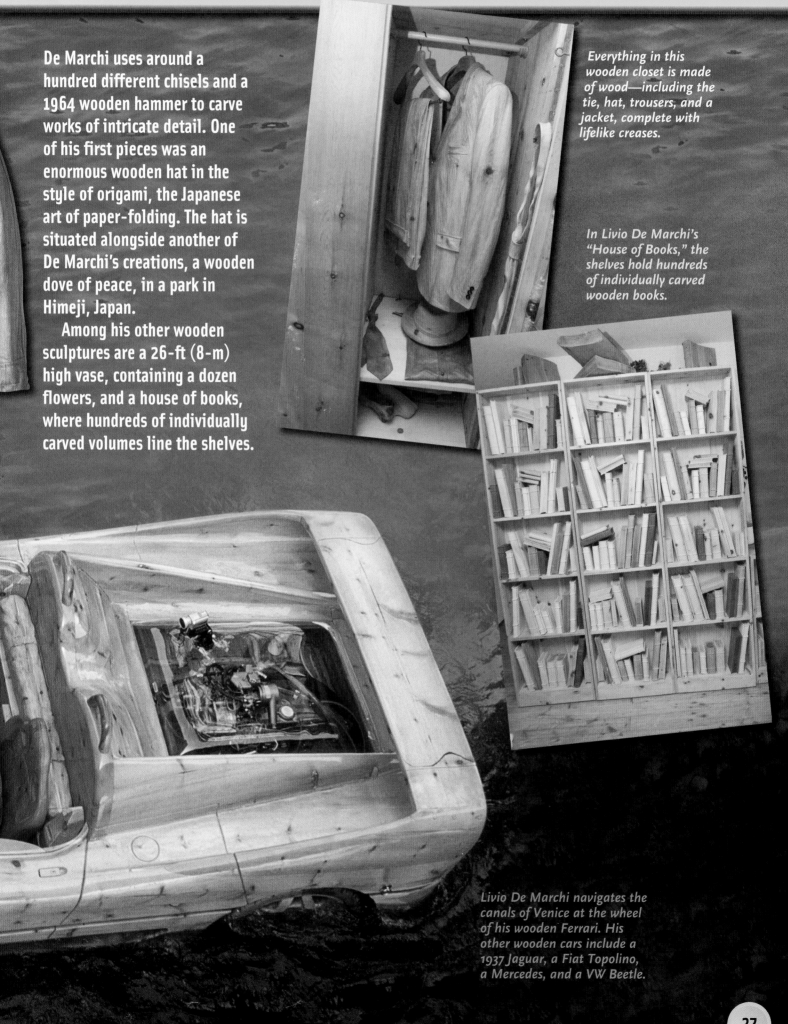

De Marchi uses around a hundred different chisels and a 1964 wooden hammer to carve works of intricate detail. One of his first pieces was an enormous wooden hat in the style of origami, the Japanese art of paper-folding. The hat is situated alongside another of De Marchi's creations, a wooden dove of peace, in a park in Himeji, Japan.

Among his other wooden sculptures are a 26-ft (8-m) high vase, containing a dozen flowers, and a house of books, where hundreds of individually carved volumes line the shelves.

Everything in this wooden closet is made of wood—including the tie, hat, trousers, and a jacket, complete with lifelike creases.

In Livio De Marchi's "House of Books," the shelves hold hundreds of individually carved wooden books.

Livio De Marchi navigates the canals of Venice at the wheel of his wooden Ferrari. His other wooden cars include a 1937 Jaguar, a Fiat Topolino, a Mercedes, and a VW Beetle.

Lion on a Leash

Whenever Jaroslav Kana ventures out from his home in the Czech Republic, he takes a walk on the wild side. Accompanying him is his pet, Leon, who is a two-year-old lion! Jaroslav obtained the lion from a private breeder two years ago and has trained him so that he will perform in advertisements and TV shows.

Rotating Car

A new Japanese electric car could make parking problems a thing of the past. The Nissan Pivo, with its 180-degree rotating cabin, always faces forward—so there's no need to reverse!

Eyes Tight Shut

Trying to moisten her eyes in January 2005, 78-year-old Australian Terry Horder accidentally grabbed the wrong bottle and glued her eyes shut. Doctors were able to get them open and her eyes were unharmed.

Roller Ride

Richard Dickson, a 37-year-old father-of-five, won a new car in May 2005 by riding the "Twister Two" roller coaster at Denver, Colorado, for nearly 53 hours, in the process covering a total of 757 mi (1,218 km).

It's **not** only your car that goes in for a wash at a **Madrid, Spain**, gas station. A coin-operated **pet-washing** machine enables animals to get *a soapy wash and dry* for approximately **$5**.

Cat Theater

Yuri Kuklachev is founder of the Moscow Cats Theater, which boasts around 30 trained housecats in its company. The cats' tricks include front-paw stands, "tightrope" walking on a pole, and traversing the pole from underneath by grasping it with four paws.

Divorce Cake

Baker Georgius Vasseliou from Berlin, Germany, has introduced a new line at his cafe—personalized divorce cakes. To celebrate a split, he has devised cakes with a large smiley face or a torn up photo of the "ex" iced on the top. And with over 10,000 divorces a year in the city, he thinks he's on to a winner.

Artistic Ape

Tama Zoo Park, in Tokyo, Japan, discovered a new talent among its residents. Gypsy, a 54-year-old orangutan, was just one of three orangutans who took to drawing with crayons. Her favorite colors were yellow and blue.

Jumping for Joy

Austrian B.A.S.E. jumper Felix Baumgartner has thrown himself off some of the world's most challenging structures—and has even mastered the art of flying.

What does B.A.S.E. mean?

❝It stands for Building, Antenna, Span (or bridge), and Earth (or cliffs). You have to jump off all four, with a parachute, to register as a B.A.S.E. jumper.❞

How did you start?

❝As a kid, I used to hang out at the airport watching the guys jumping out of airplanes, and as soon as I was 16, and could get my parachute license, I started skydiving. Ten years later, I made my first B.A.S.E. jump from a bridge in West Virginia, and a year after that I had become the first European to win the international championships.❞

What is the highest jump you have made?

❝The Petronas Towers in Kuala Lumpur in 1999. At the time they were the highest buildings in the world, and hard to get into—my preparations took two months. I put my parachute and a hand-held camera in a little suitcase and sneaked to the 88th floor disguised as a businessman. I climbed onto a window-cleaning platform and jumped from 451 m— eight seconds in freefall at 170 km/h before the parachute opened.❞

What is the lowest jump you have ever made?

❝The Christ the Redeemer statue in Rio de Janeiro. I saw it on a documentary and thought the right arm was far out over the mountain and that it would be a high jump—in fact I had just 29 m, which gave me only 1½ seconds to open the parachute. I didn't want to sneak up the inside stairs, so I used a crossbow to shoot an arrow over the right arm with a steel cable attached and pulled myself up. I stepped off the 25-cm wide hand and pictures of it went across the world.❞

When and where did you learn to "fly"?

❝In 2003, I was the first person to "fly" across the English Channel unaided. I have always dreamed of flying—we spent years preparing, with a team of 40 people working on different types of wings. Eventually, we found the perfect wing—a 6-ft carbon-fiber fin—and I jumped out of a plane over Dover at 30,000 ft and "flew" 22 mi at speeds of up to 225 mph until I reached the other side.❞

Did you fear you might not make it?

❝There was a big chance of losing my life if something went wrong with the oxygen tank I was wearing. At that altitude you need every breath, and if there's no oxygen you die in less than a minute. But I was well-prepared—I trained in a wind tunnel, and was even strapped onto the roof of a Porsche car speeding down an airport runway to see how it feels at that speed.❞

Was it the scariest thing you've done?

❝No. That was jumping into the Mamet cave in Croatia's Velebit National Park. Usually I can see when I jump, but that was totally dark and I had to use an MP3 player to give a countdown of when I'd get to the bottom, 190 m down at 170 km/h.❞

What makes you jump—and how long will you carry on?

❝I like to be in the air—it's like my second home. I have made more than 2,600 parachute jumps and 130 B.A.S.E. jumps, and I think I'll be doing it for a long while yet.❞

No Ordinary Chimp

Charlie the chimpanzee is a black belt at karate! The 17-year-old chimp, who weighs 200 lb (90 kg) and stands 4½ ft (1.4 m) tall, is seen here practicing with his owner Carmen Presti of Niagara Falls, New York.

Time Warp

A gas-station manager in Lincoln, Nebraska, accidentally turned back the clock 50 years in October 2005 by selling premium gasoline for 32 cents a gallon instead of the usual $3.20. Drivers could hardly believe their luck as they pulled into Kabredlo's Convenience Store. The mistake with the decimal point was corrected after 45 minutes.

Satanic Turtle

For Bryan and Marsha Dora, Lucky the turtle is the devil in a half-shell. The only survivor of a fierce fire that killed 150 other animals at their pet shop in Frankfort, Indiana, in 2005, the red-eared slider turtle emerged from the inferno with the face of the devil on his shell. The heat gave the shell a new pattern, with Satanic eyes, lips, goatee, and devil's horns.

Baby Driver

A four-year-old boy drove his mother's car on a late-night trip to a video store. Although he was too small to reach the accelerator, the boy put the car into gear and the idling engine took him to the store 400 yd (370 m) away in Sand Lake, Michigan. Unfortunately, the video store was shut and on his return journey the youngster hit two parked cars, and then reversed into a police car. His mother said that he had learned how to drive the car while sitting on her lap.

Flushed Fish
Some of the oldest public bathrooms in Paris, France, have been transformed into havens of wacky chic by introducing live goldfish into the fake plumbing!

Lofty View
Katya Davidson had a different view of the world than most people—the 15-year-old walked about her house on 32-in (80-cm) stilts, jumped rope on a bouncy ball 3 ft (1 m) high, and unicycled down to her local grocery store in Roseville, California. Her love of circus apparatus began when she was aged nine, and she got her first unicycle for Christmas.

Street Skiing
Olympic ski champion Jonny Moseley helped transform one of San Francisco's streets into the venue for a king-of-the-hill contest in September 2005. Trucked-in snow was dumped on two blocks of Fillmore Street, a section so steep that the sidewalks have staircases. The skiers raced down the run, which measured 400 ft (120 m).

On **November 25, 2004,** a robber took **$14,500** from a bank in FUKUOKA, JAPAN, but was so **overcome with guilt** that he *mailed the money back* with an **apology note** a week later!

Pension Imposter

After a Turkish mother died in 2003, her 47-year-old son, Serafettin Gencel, buried her in his basement and disguised himself as her for the following two years so that he could collect her retirement pension. He regularly visited the bank dressed in a woman's overcoat, headscarf, and stockings, until employees became suspicious of his voice.

Serafettin Gencel, dressed as his dead mother, sitting in the bank where he drew her pension.

Pug Dressers
In Naples, Florida, there is an annual beauty contest, although it is not for people but for pug dogs. The Pug o'ween event was started in 1998 by pug-owner Karen Coplin for those who like to dress up their pugs in fancy costumes.

Still Alive
Dona Ramona, from Sampues, Colombia, was still very much alive in October 2005, despite being wrongly declared dead on four separate occasions. Doctors defended their prognoses, saying that they were fooled because the 97-year-old kept slipping into a diabetic coma.

▶ Cyclops

A kitten named Cy, short for Cyclops, was born on December 28, 2005, in Redmond, Oregon, with only one eye and no nose. A ragdoll breed, sadly it survived for only a few hours.

Kicking Out

Twelve-year-old Michael Hoffman, a taekwondo black belt from Ann Arbor, Michigan, managed to kick a cushioned pad 2,377 times in a single hour in October 2005. He alternated between using his right and left leg every minute.

Key to Success

After a joke backfired and Arthur Richardson, of North Platte, Nebraska, ended up swallowing the key to his friend's truck, a doctor X-rayed Richardson's stomach and said that the key posed no danger to his health. But his friend still needed to use the truck. So they took the X rays to locksmith John Somers, who used the pictures to fashion a new key. Amazingly it worked in the truck!

Sand Painting

In October 2005, 70 schoolchildren created a sand portrait measuring 85 x 59 ft (26 x 18 m) on the beach at Scarborough, England. The portrait of Lord Nelson and the HMS *Victory* celebrated the 200th anniversary of the Battle of Trafalgar. They used half a ton of pigment, a quarter of a ton of sand, and over a mile of string to create the sand painting in ten different colors. Painting began at 9.30 a.m. and had to be completed before high tide at 7 p.m.

Slow Way

Paul Kramer took the slow way to his niece's wedding. He hopped onto his bicycle at his home in southern California on April 12, 2005, and pulled into his brother's driveway at North Olmsted, Ohio, 71 days and 4,250 mi (6,840 km) later.

Honey Trap

An estimated one million bees were living inside the walls of St. Mark's United Church of Christ in Knox, Pennsylvania, in 2005. The problem became so serious that honey was oozing through the walls!

The entire town of **KIRUNA, SWEDEN,** is being relocated at a cost of more than **$2.5 billion** to save it from *sliding* into the abandoned iron mines below.

Hypnotic Robber

A crook in Moldova found a new way of robbing banks in 2005—he put cashiers into a trance before making them hand over the money. With the hypnotist still at large, the country's bank clerks were warned not to make eye contact with customers.

Pigeon Fancier

In 2005, a Los Angeles, California, man was found to be sharing his house with 300 birds—dead and alive—including 120 dead pigeons. The man was reportedly often seen walking with his favorite pigeon.

◀ Inverted Feet

Wang Fang, from Chongqing, China, has inverted feet. She can still walk and run and successfully manages her own restaurant business.

▶ **Underwater Juggling**
American performer Ashrita Furman juggles in an aquatheater in Kuala Lumpur among nurse sharks and 3,000 other marine animals. His personal best is juggling continuously for 37 minutes and 45 seconds at a depth of more than 13 ft (4 m).

Index

ACKNOWLEDGMENTS

COVER (t/l) Czech News Agency/Empics, (b/l) Israel Sun/Rex Features, (t/r) www.humancannonball.us, (b/r) Livio De Marchi; 4 Livio De Marchi; 6 www.24thcid.com; 7 (t/l), (t/r) & (b/r) www.24thcid.com, (b/l) Camera Press/ED/CB; 8 (t) Czech News Agency/Empics, (b) Richard Crease/Rex Features; 9 Israel Sun/Rex Features; 10 Jean-Christophe Verhaegen/Reuters; 11 (t) Rex Features, (b) Tao-Chuan Yeh/ AFP/Getty Images; 12 (l) Jorge Silva/Reuters, (r) Norman Kent/Jump for the Cause/Reuters; 13 Jeff J Mitchell/Reuters; 14 Ognen Teofilovski/ Reuters; 15 (t) Jay Cheng/Reuters, (b) National Taiwan University/Reuters; 16 (t) Marsha Ruff, (b/l) & (b/r) John Gomes/The Alaska Zoo; 17 David Gray/Reuters; 20 (t) Bogdan Cristel/Reuters; 21 Mark Lennihan/AP/PA Photos; 22 Alastair Grant/Empics; 23 www.humancannonball.us; 26 (t) & (dp) Livio De Marchi, (b/l) Barcroft Media; 27 (t/r) & (c/r) Barcroft Media; 28 (t) Czech News Agency/Empics; (b) Noboru Hashimoto/ Reuters; 29 Reuters; 30 (t/l & t/r) Sam Barcroft/Rex Features; 31 (t/l) & (t/r) Xavier Lhospice/Reuters, (b) IHLAS News Agency/Reuters; 32 (t) Traci Allen/Empics; (b) Chinafotopress/Camera Press; 33 Vincent Thian/Empics

All other photos are from Corel, PhotoDisc, Digital Vision and Ripley's Entertainment Inc.